The Orchard Book of Stories from
ANCIENT EGYPT

For Martin and Sinead
RS

To Jill Lambert, with love
SL

In the same series

THE ORCHARD BOOK OF GREEK MYTHS
Retold by Geraldine McCaughrean
Illustrated by Emma Chichester Clark

THE ORCHARD BOOK OF GREEK GODS AND GODDESSES
Retold by Geraldine McCaughrean
Illustrated by Emma Chichester Clark

THE ORCHARD BOOK OF VIKINGS
Retold by Robert Swindells
Illustrated by Peter Utton

THE ORCHARD BOOK OF ROMAN MYTHS
Retold by Geraldine McCaughrean
Illustrated by Emma Chichester Clark

ORCHARD BOOKS
338 Euston Road, London NW1 3BH
Orchard Books Australia
Hachette Children's Books
Level 17/207 Kent Street, Sydney, NSW 2000
ISBN 1 84362 306 4
First published in Great Britain in 2000
This edition published in 2003
Text © Robert Swindells 2000
Illustrations © Stephen Lambert 2000
The rights of Robert Swindells to be identified as the author and of
Stephen Lambert to be identified as the illustrator of this work have been asserted by them
in accordance with the Copyright, Designs and Patents Act, 1988.
A CIP catalogue record for this book is available from the British Library.
3 5 7 9 10 8 6 4 2
Printed in Singapore

The Orchard Book
of Stories from
ANCIENT
EGYPT

Retold by Robert Swindells
Illustrated by Stephen Lambert

ORCHARD BOOKS

CONTENTS

CONTENTS

INTRODUCTION

*L*ong long ago, in the time before Pharaohs and mummies and pyramids, there lived in the land of Egypt a race of hunter-gatherers. They lived in small groups which were forever fighting one another. When times were particularly hard these first Egyptians sometimes even ate each other. They lived on a broad strip of fertile land which lay along the banks of a great river called the Nile. Beyond this fertile strip, pressing in on both sides, was the desert, a seemingly endless ocean of shifting, sun-blasted sand where nothing grew and no creature could survive.

Two things kept the people of Egypt alive: the river, which flooded once a year to spread a layer of rich black silt across the strip, and the sun, which shone down on the wild fruits and grains in the silt and caused them to grow. The river-banks, with their lush stands of papyrus reed, teemed with birds and animals which ate these fruits and grains, and which in turn were eaten by the hunters.

As time went on, the Egyptians learned how to till the soil and grow crops in it. They began to domesticate animals too, so that gradually they ceased to be hunter-gatherers and became farmers instead. Life became a little easier. People didn't need to roam about as much to find their food. They started building permanent homes instead of temporary shelters. They still hunted sometimes but now it was mostly for sport, and they never had to eat one another. Their settlements became villages, then towns, then cities, but they still depended on the river and the sun to keep their farmland fertile. Without these recurrent miracles their lives would not be possible.

Because of this, Egyptians began asking themselves how all the wonders around them began. How did the sun get into the sky, what drives it across the heavens and where does it go at night? Who made the Nile and who causes its annual flood? Where did trees and grass and flowers come from? How did we begin?

There were no scientists in those days, so these matters could not be investigated. Instead the people made up stories to explain the mysteries which puzzled them. The stories were about gods and goddesses and all sorts of magic. The Egyptians wrote them down in their beautiful hieroglyphic script, sometimes carving them into the walls of the temples they erected to the glory of these gods and goddesses, and of the tombs of their kings. These temples and tombs were the mightiest structures ever erected by human hands, and the civilisation which created them was the most advanced, the most powerful on earth. It flourished for over three thousand years and when it crumbled, its pyramids and gigantic statues did not. They stood two thousand years in the sand, objects of wonder to all who viewed them, the meanings of their inscriptions forgotten. Two thousand years, till somebody unearthed a chunk of basalt known as the Rosetta Stone which unlocked the secret of the hieroglyphs. Stories unread for millennia were restored to the world. Some of them are in this book.

The Light and Life of all Things

How it all began

*T*here was a time, many thousands of years ago, when there was no earth, no sky, no light. There were no oceans, rivers or mountains, no trees or grass or animals, and of course no people. There was nothing but a mass of black, heaving water which stretched for ever and had no life. The only thing that existed in this lightless chaos was a spirit: the nameless spirit of a formless mass. One day it occurred to the spirit to give itself a name. *Khepera*, it rumbled in a voice like thunder, and was transformed at once into the form of a mighty god.

Now the word Khepera means 'he who becomes the light and life of all things' and that is exactly what Khepera set out to do. First he created a great shining egg which rocked and bobbed on the face of the deep. From this egg sprang *Ra*, a god even mightier than his father Khepera. The first thing Ra did was to command earth and sky to rise out of the water. The earth he called *Geb*, the sky was *Nut*. To separate them Ra created *Shu*, called the uplifter. Nut placed her toes at the eastern horizon and her fingertips at the western horizon so that her gigantic body formed an arch over the earth. Nut's body and limbs were studded with sparkling gems which became the stars.

Every morning Ra would board his boat and set sail across the sky, gazing down at the earth with an eye so huge and bright that it saw everything that was happening below. Ra's eye was the sun, the source of all light, and he was proud of it. He was stunned when he returned one day from his voyage across the sky and found that Khepera had got hold of a second eye. The new eye burned far less brightly than his own, but the sun-god was livid all the same.

"You've got *my* eye," he yelled at his father. "Why do you need another one?"

Now Khepera didn't enjoy being shouted at by his own son, so to serve Ra right he decreed that this new eye would be called *Thoth*, and that it would light up the sky whenever Ra couldn't be there. Furthermore it would have the title Measurer of Time. Ra flew into a rage but it did no good. Khepera's decree meant that the moon, which is what the second eye was, would be used for ever to calculate the lengths of months.

Khepera went on to create six more gods, each with special duties to perform. This done, he created men and women and placed them on the earth so that they might worship him. He caused trees to grow, and grasses, and every sort of plant. He created fishes and reptiles, birds and animals, and when he had done all these things, he rested. And *that*, said the Egyptians, is how it all began.

Unruly Children

Nut and Geb

With Khepera living in retirement somewhere beyond the sky, Ra was in charge of just about everything. He was always busy. Each morning while it was still dark, he had to climb into his boat and set off down the Celestial Nile. This was a river like the Nile which flowed through Egypt, except that this one flowed across the sky.

As Ra's boat nosed out towards midstream, rays of light from the god's mighty eye shone down on the sleeping earth, warming the soil and rousing all creatures from their slumbers. It was time for day to begin. As the boat sailed on, the light grew brighter, more fierce, till it became impossible for anyone on earth to look at it. Its heat became so intense that in the middle of the day people had to seek whatever shade they could find to keep from being burned, and it was woe betide anybody unlucky enough to be lost in the desert, where there was no shade.

Ra's voyage from east to west took all day, and when evening came he couldn't relax, because when the Celestial Nile reached

the mountains of the west it became a great cataract or waterfall, plunging down, down into a thundering black abyss called Tuat. Ra did not fall with his boat over this cataract, but he had to leave part of his spirit in the vessel to help the souls of the newly dead who would clamber aboard from the roaring foam at the foot of the falls. Ra himself stepped out on to the Fields of Peace, which lie beyond the sky. This is where Khepera lived, and many other gods, but there was no peace for Ra. He had to spend the night sitting on a golden throne, dispensing justice and directing events in heaven and on earth. It was a hectic life, being the sun-god.

Ra had four children: two girls and two boys. The girls were called Nut and Tefnut, the boys were Shu and Geb. One day, without asking their father, Nut and Geb got married. It was quite usual in Egypt for sisters

and brothers to wed, but Ra was furious when he found out. "You *dare*," he roared, "you *dare* marry without my permission? I'll show *you*!"

He knew that they'd married because Nut wanted to have a baby. In fact she was desperate for one, so Ra put a cruel curse on the couple.

"The day will never dawn," he thundered, "when a child will be born to you." Dawn was one of the things he was in charge of.

Nut was distraught.

"Father," she cried, "ever since you created the earth I have stood with my toes on the eastern horizon and my fingertips on the western horizon. Without me there'd be no sky. No stars at night. I perform faithfully the task you set me, yet you deny me that which every young wife desires: a child of her own."

She begged and pleaded but it was no use – Ra turned from her,
muttering about disobedience and its consequences, so the young bride
made a cunning plan. She'd heard that the god Thoth, whose eye was the
moon and who was a scribe in the Underworld, was fond of a game of
dice. Now Thoth was pretty powerful, and one of his titles was Measurer
of Time. So one day Nut popped into the Underworld to talk to Thoth.

"If we have a game of dice," she said, "and I beat you, what will you
give me?"

Thoth laughed. He hardly ever lost at dice. "If you beat *me*," he chuckled,
"you can have anything you want."

So he got the dice out and they played. Nut used a bit of magic, which
was cheating really, but Thoth was enjoying the game so much he didn't
notice and before he knew it, he'd lost.

"Hmmm," he mumbled. "I don't know how *that* happened, but I promised you anything you wanted and a promise is a promise, so what's it to be?"

"I want you to stick five extra days on the end of each year," said Nut. The Egyptian year had three hundred and sixty days.

Thoth looked at her. "You want me to make the *year* longer?"

"Yes." Nut nodded. "You're Measurer of Time, aren't you?"

Thoth nodded.

"Well it'll be easy for you then, won't it?"

So Thoth added five days to the end of each year, and because these days weren't on the calendar, Ra had no control over them. His curse had no power, and it was on these days that the children of Nut and Geb were born. Like Ra, the couple had two girls and two boys. The girls were called Isis and Nephthys. The boys were Osiris and Seth. Ra was seriously upset at the way these babies kept coming along, but he couldn't prevent it. His daughter had outmanoeuvred him and what was worse she'd done it with the help of Thoth, his rival; that despised second eye in the sky. So Ra sulked, said he'd have nothing more to do with earthly matters and stamped off to live in the sky.

A LAKE OF BLOOD

How Ra punished his people

*W*ith Ra now spending most of his time in the sky, people started to forget that it was he who made the world.

"Why should we do as *he* says," they muttered, "he's never here. Why don't we get rid of him and choose a king of our own?"

Ra still had friends in Egypt though, and he soon got to know that the people were plotting against him. He called the gods and goddesses to an urgent meeting. "There's a plot," he told them, "a plot by the people to overthrow me and put somebody else in my place." He frowned. "I'm the one who *made* them, and now they want to be rid of me. What d'you think I should do – punish, or forgive?"

None of the gods or goddesses wanted the people forgiven.

"We are gods," they spluttered, "and they are only people. How *dare* they plot against us? You should send your eye to wreak revenge upon them."

Ra's mighty eye was the sun, but it could take on other shapes as well. Now, at Ra's command, it took on the form of a savage lioness.

Ra looked at the fearsome cat. "Go to earth," he hissed. "Go to earth and kill. Kill, and kill, and kill. Don't stop killing till the last human is dead. Go now."

The lioness needed no urging. She loved to kill. Blood was her favourite drink. With a terrible roar she leapt down on to the earth and began tearing people to pieces, seizing and shaking them till bones snapped and blood spurted. She didn't eat her victims; there wasn't time. No sooner had she shaken the life out of one than she was bounding after another. People fled in all directions, shrieking for mercy and trying to hide, but the dreadful beast had a keen nose: wherever they hid she sniffed them out. By the end of the day she'd slaughtered half the people on earth. As darkness fell she returned to Ra's palace, and the god gave her a name: *Sekhmet*, which means powerful.

"You have done well, Sekhmet," he purred. "You can stop now – the people will never dare plot against me again."

The lioness gazed at him. "*Till the last human is dead*, you said. I'll finish the job tomorrow." Not even the word of Ra could quell Sekhmet's blood-lust.

Ra's anger had cooled. Now he felt sorry for the people who were left. He couldn't stop thinking about the awful fate they would suffer tomorrow.

"I must stop the lioness," he told himself. "I must think up some sort of trick."

An idea came to him. In the south of Egypt there is a particular sort of stone which is red. In the middle of the night, Ra whispered to the high priest of his temple at Heliopolis, and the high priest sent men to gather great chunks of this stone. At the same time, he commanded the women of the temple to brew seven thousand jars of beer. When the stone arrived it was ground to a fine powder which was added to the beer. The beer now looked like blood. Ra ordered all seven thousand jars to be poured on to the ground, where it formed a dark red lake.

When Sekhmet leapt down on to the earth at dawn, the first thing she saw was the lake.

"Blood," she growled, "and I don't even have to chase it." She crouched on the rim of the lake and began to lap. She meant to drink the place dry before starting on the people, but soon she had so much beer inside her that she became falling-down drunk. She forgot what she was supposed to be doing, and if she'd remembered she wouldn't have cared. She lapped till she couldn't make her tongue do what she wanted it to any more, then she got up and staggered back to Ra's palace, muttering and giggling to herself. Next day she had the world's biggest headache, and by the time that went away she'd forgotten all about killing people. Ra, pleased with the success of his clever trick, took great care not to remind her.

As for the people, they knew who had saved their lives and never plotted against Ra again.

THE GIFTS OF THE GODS

Isis and Osiris

*T*here are two sorts of people in the world – the lucky and the unlucky, and it was just the same in ancient Egypt. When the children of Nut and Geb grew up, Isis and Osiris were given the fertile land of Egypt to rule, while Seth and Nephthys reigned over what was left, which was mostly desert.

So Isis and Osiris were the lucky ones, but they had a great deal of work to do. The land was good but the people were virtual savages. Instead of growing crops and keeping herds and flocks, they got their meat by hunting animals in the marshes, and ate roots and berries gathered from trees or dug out of the soil with sharpened sticks. Sometimes they raided the nests of wild bees to steal honey and were badly stung in the process. There was never enough food, and bands of wandering hunters would often clash, fighting over a handful of seeds or the carcass of an animal. People were killed or wounded in these squabbles, and many of the wounded died because there was no knowledge of medicine or healing. From time to time, when food was really scarce, human flesh was eaten.

Isis and Osiris were good, wise rulers. They did not approve of the way the Egyptians lived. Isis was particularly revolted by their occasional cannibalism, so she confronted them and said, "It is very wrong of you to eat the flesh of your fellow humans, no matter how hungry you are. If you will pay attention to the things Osiris and I can show you, I promise you will always have enough to eat without eating each other."

The people watched as Osiris showed them where useful metals lay hidden in the earth. "With these metals you can make ploughs and hoes and sickles with which to work the soil," he said. "Copper's best for this. Gold's too soft, but it makes beautiful brooches and bangles."

Then Isis showed them how they might plant seeds and keep sheep and goats and cattle. "Do these things," she said, "and there will be enough food for everybody without the need to hunt or scrabble for roots."

She showed them how to make hives for bees to live in, and how to collect their honey without being stung. Now the people had milk and meat, honey and corn, right there beside their houses. They didn't have to forage. There was no need to fight.

"Hey," they cried, "this is a lot better than the old ways."

Now that they had learned to live together in peace, Isis and Osiris taught the Egyptians which herbs were good for healing, how to spin and weave, how to grind corn and bake the flour to make bread. They taught the art of working in stone, and the Egyptians used this knowledge to build elaborate temples in honour of gentle Isis and Osiris the wise. In the fullness of time great cities grew up around these temples: cities whose populations wore fine clothes and exquisite jewellery of gold and precious stones. Outside the cities lay neat fertile farms tended by well-fed, mostly happy peasants, proud of their magnificent country and its empire of conquered lands.

Thus, under the reign of Isis, and of Osiris whom the people called the Good One, there blossomed from a savage past the greatest civilisation the world had ever known.

THE BEAUTIFUL BOX

The death of Osiris

While Isis and Osiris were busy transforming Egypt, their brother Seth was sulking in the desert.

"Why is it," he growled, "that everybody loves Osiris and nobody loves me?"

His wife smiled. "That's easy, Seth. Osiris has turned Egypt into a beautiful land, where people live together in peace. They have nice houses and good clothes and plenty to eat. In the meantime all you've done is skulk about in the desert, moaning. You haven't improved the place at all. It's still dry and hot, with snakes and scorpions and sand that blows about, getting into everything. People *die* out here."

"Yes, but he got the best bit," grumbled Seth. "The bit with the Nile in it. If I'd got that part, *I'd* have made it beautiful. There's nothing clever about fixing a place up when there's water. I could do wonders with this desert if there was a river running through it."

"If there was a river it wouldn't be a desert," said Nephthys.

Seth glared at her. "Don't try to be smart," he growled. "It doesn't suit you."

Nephthys smiled and left the room without another word. She was used to her husband's moods. When she had gone, Seth settled down to a good long brood. He enjoyed brooding and besides, there wasn't much else to do in the desert.

I'll show them, he thought. I'll teach them to love my brother and hate me. I'll get rid of him, do him in, then I'll be king of Egypt. There won't be a lot of feasting and dancing and swanning about in fancy kit then, I can tell you.

He thought up a trick. A really cruel trick. It was so good he laughed out loud, but he daren't tell his wife. Nephthys loved her sister Isis, and she was quite fond of Osiris too. If he shared his brilliant idea with her she'd probably shoot off and warn them.

Now Seth knew that his brother had just returned from a long journey and was resting in the city of Memphis. Probably showing off about all the places he's seen, he thought. Stay right where you are, Brother. Don't go away. I've got a surprise for you.

By trickery, Seth had got hold of his brother's exact measurements. Now he took them to the best carpenter he knew and said, "I want you to make me a box someone this size can lie down in. Put plenty of fancy carving on the outside, with gold leaf and lapis-lazuli and all like that. I don't want any old rubbish. It's a present for a very special friend. Oh — and make it airtight so anybody trapped inside will suffocate."

He went home and ordered his seventy-two scruffy followers to start preparing a lavish banquet. As they got busy, Seth had his chariot brought round and headed for Memphis, where he was shown into his brother's presence. He strode smiling across the marble floor, flung his arms round Osiris and hugged him.

"Welcome back, Brother," Seth boomed. "Everybody's missed you, including me and Nephthys. In fact we've arranged a little feast tonight in your honour, if you can spare the time."

Osiris said of course he could spare the time. It was so kind of Seth to lay on a banquet just for him. He'd be there around seven.

The banquet was a great success. There was music, every kind of delicious food, the finest wines. There were dancers and tumblers and fire-eaters and sumptuous couches to sprawl on. Everybody was having a wonderful time when, at a signal from Seth, his followers carried in the most magnificent box the revellers had ever set eyes on. It was huge. It was ornate. It gleamed with gold. It flashed and glittered as its thousand inlaid gems caught the light, reflecting it back in spangles of blue, green and ruby. Osiris gazed at the beautiful object, hoping it was a gift from his brother to him.

"Now, everybody." Seth had risen to his feet to get their attention. "We're going to play a little game."

"Oooh," went the happy guests, and "Aaah!" Some clapped their hands.

Their host smiled and nodded. "The name of the game is, 'The One that Fits It, Gits It'."

Everybody laughed except Osiris, who was disappointed. Oh, he thought, so it *isn't* for me. It was, but not the way he'd hoped.

How the game was played was, everybody took turns at climbing into the box and lying down. Seth's followers peered over the rim each time to see whether the guest fitted the box, but nobody did. One or two were too big, but most were not tall enough. With their heads touching one end, they couldn't touch the other with their feet. There were groans of disappointment. Everybody longed to own the magnificent box.

Presently it was Osiris' turn. He was excited. I'm quite tall, he thought. Perhaps I'll turn out to be the lucky one. He clambered into the box, lay down and wriggled about a bit. With the top of his head touching one end, his heels touched the other. The width was exactly right too, snug to his broad shoulders.

"Yesss!" he cried, but before he could rise and claim his prize, Seth's followers slammed down the lid and sat on it. Stout ropes were fetched. As these were passed under the box, tugged tight and knotted, the guests could hear Osiris kicking and hammering and hollering inside, but they were all Seth's friends. Isis hadn't been invited to the banquet and nobody else was interested in helping the king.

The box, with its hapless occupant, was carried outside and heaved into the waters of the Nile. The current caught it and whirled it away while the followers of Seth stood cheering on the bank. Osiris, dead from suffocation, was gone at last and their jealous leader was able to seize the throne of Egypt.

THE EVIL TYRANT

Isis forced to flee

*T*error stalked the land of Egypt. Seth was as cruel on the throne as he had been miserable off it. He set his seventy-two scruffy followers to hunting down and putting to death all who had been friends with Osiris. Everybody was suspect. Nobody felt safe. Even the gods were scared. Some of them changed themselves into the shapes of animals and took to living in holes and caves in order to fool the followers of Seth. Isis, weeping in her rooms over the loss of her beloved husband, was in the most terrible danger. She was expecting a baby. It was Osiris' baby, the rightful heir to the throne. If Seth found out this child was on its way, he'd have Isis murdered at once. The god Thoth was desperate to prevent this. He came under cover of darkness to see her.

"Good Queen," he said, "the child you carry inside your body is Egypt's only hope. You must flee."

"Where?" asked Isis. "Everybody knows my face. I'd be betrayed. Seth's men would capture me in no time."

The god shook his head. "Not if you hide in the delta. Think of its thousand islands, those twisted waterways, the marshes with their dense vegetation. Only those who are born there can find their way through the delta of the Nile."

"But …" The queen's lip quivered. "I don't know anybody there. I'd be all alone."

Thoth nodded gravely. "That is for the best, good Queen. If nobody knows you're there, nobody can betray you. Look." The god snapped his fingers and seven scorpions came creeping across the floor. "Take these creatures with you. Their deadly stings will discourage the curious and they're company of a sort. It's the best I can do."

So poor Isis slipped away from the home she'd shared with Osiris, and headed for the Nile delta with the seven scorpions scuttling at her heels.

She travelled quickly, knowing she must be deep among the reedbeds by the time Ra's fiery sun-boat began its voyage across the sky. If some frightened Egyptian spotted her, he might betray her to Seth in the hope of pleasing the cruel king.

She made it just in time. As the mighty Ra stepped aboard his boat in the eastern sky, the unhappy queen slipped into the delta's chill shadows. She was safe for now, but she must find a place to stay. A place to bear her child – the child Thoth had called Egypt's only hope. And she must think of a way to equip her baby with special powers. Magic powers, which would be desperately needed if the child was someday to depose the evil tyrant now squatting toadlike on his country's throne.

The Secret Name

How Isis tricked Ra

*T*he mighty sun-god Ra had a secret name with unbelievable magic powers. Anybody who managed to find out Ra's secret name would have these powers too. Trouble was, Ra had a number of names besides the secret one. Sometimes he was known as Amon, sometimes Ptah and sometimes Khephri. It depended where the person was who was speaking about him, what time of day it was and many other things. Nobody ever called Ra by his secret name though, because nobody knew what it was. Ra kept it strictly to himself.

Isis sat in the shade of a papyrus clump, watching the brown water flow sluggishly by. The followers of Seth were searching for her all over Egypt but she was safe here in the delta, at least for now. Soon her baby would be born, but before he arrived she must find the powerful magic he would someday need in his battle against Seth. "What I need," she mused, "is the magic in Ra's secret name. If *only* I could think of a way to make him tell me what that name is."

Now Isis possessed powers of sorcery, and she used them to fly to the Fields of Peace where Ra lived with many other gods, and where the souls of the dead tilled soil which was always fertile, producing crops which never failed.

I'll hide myself near where he walks, she thought, and spy on him. Who knows – perhaps he'll say his secret name to himself and I'll overhear.

So she concealed herself in dense shrubbery beside Ra's favourite footpath and spied on him as he passed by. Sometimes he muttered to himself as he walked near her hiding place, sometimes he'd be humming a tune, but he never spoke his secret name.

Isis almost despaired, then one day as the sun-god drew level with her hiding place he spat on the ground. Isis decided it was time to employ a little more of her sorcery. She waited till Ra ambled out of sight round a bend, then crept out and mixed his spit with the dust it had fallen on.

This produced a glob of mud, which the sorceress moulded into the shape of a snake. She mumbled some magic words over the snake, which promptly came to life. Isis hid the snake under some stones on the path, and slipped back into the bushes.

After a short time Ra returned. As he walked past the stones he felt a stabbing pain in his toe. He let out a startled cry and hopped around, holding his foot. As other gods came running to see what was the matter, Ra stopped hopping and fell to the ground where he lay gasping and writhing, racked with pain. His skin, bathed in a cold sweat, took on a bluish tinge. The snake had slithered away unnoticed but its venom was spreading through Ra's body. The gods looked on aghast, wondering what vile disease had felled the sun-god, for they could see he was dying.

It was then that Isis stepped out of the bushes.

"He has been bitten by a snake," she rapped, kneeling by Ra's head. She looked into his eyes. "Tell me your secret name, and I will say words to make the venom harmless."

Ra was in agony, but he was determined to guard his secret. "My name is Ra," he gasped.

"No!" cried Isis. "Your *secret* name."

"It is Amon."

Isis shook her head.

"Khephri."

She shook her head again.

"Ptah."

Isis bent over the shivering god.

"You haven't much time," she hissed. "So you'd better stop playing around."

Ra gazed up at the sorceress through haunted eyes.

"All right, all right," he croaked, "come closer – nobody else must hear."

With the last of his strength he mumbled the secret name in Isis' ear.

Isis nodded, smiled and straightened up. The gods were watching anxiously from a distance. She fixed her eyes on Ra's and spoke the magic words. At once the venom in the god's body turned to water. He stopped gasping and lay still. The pain was fading. He could breathe more easily. The light was coming back.

As Ra sat up, Isis rose to her feet. The gods were hurrying forward with cries of relief and she thought, You are gods and I am only a sorceress, but I know something now which none of you knows, and it has made me more powerful than all of you put together. Now I have something of value to hand on to my unborn child.

She uttered a spell, and in a flash she had left the Fields of Peace and was back in the Nile delta, under the shadow of the papyrus, awaiting the birth of her baby.

THE LITTLE SWALLOW

Isis searches for Osiris

*T*he sun hung blazing in a copper-coloured sky. Isis lay very still in her little pool of shadow. She knew that the sun was the eye of Ra, and that the mighty god was seeking her, angry that she had stolen his secret name. It was as she lay there, watching Ra's progress across the heavens, that her baby was born. The child was a boy, and Isis called him Horus.

He was a strong, healthy child and Isis was very happy, except when she remembered the perilous task he'd been born to perform. "How I wish your life might be blessed with peace," she whispered, but she knew that inside his tiny body he carried the power she had taken from Ra. She smiled bravely and said, "One day, my little one, you must seize the throne of Egypt and avenge your poor dead father. Only *then* will you know peace – you, and Egypt."

Thinking of Osiris sent a pang of sorrow through Isis' heart. If only she knew where his body lay she might prevail on the gods to let him live again, then her happiness would be complete. He was cast adrift on the Nile, she thought. The box could be somewhere here, in the delta. I could leave Horus sleeping in the shade, protected by one of my spells, while I search.

Isis cast a spell so that her baby would sleep in safety till she returned. She was a shape-changer, so she took the form of a swallow and soared into the sky. Now I can look down and see the whole delta, she thought. My search will be brief.

For once, though, the sorceress was wrong. The beautiful box containing her husband's body had drifted far across the sea and had been washed up on the coast of distant Phoenicia. There, by a sort of miracle, the wood it was made of had come to life, sprouting roots and branches. Soon it had become a great tree. There was nothing to show that it had once been something else, because the box lay deep within its mighty trunk.

One day the king of Phoenicia spotted the lovely tree and ordered it to be felled. "Carve a great pillar from it," he commanded, "and erect it in my palace."

So, while poor Isis rode the sky in ever-widening circles, the tree with her husband's body inside became a beautifully carved column in the palace of the Phoenician king.

It was a long time before the little swallow reached the shores of Phoenicia. She had to keep returning to the delta to see that Horus was safe and well, but presently Isis found herself swooping over a magnificent palace. Her magic powers told her something she could scarcely believe – it seemed her husband's body was inside one of the pillars which supported the roof of this palace. How can this be, she wondered, but she glided to earth, took her own shape and set about getting inside the palace.

This was not easy. The doors were guarded at all times. When a pretty stranger approached with some wild tale about searching for her husband's body the guards laughed, thinking her mad.

"Oh aye, love," they chuckled, "the whole place is built out of dead husbands. Widows come here all the time asking for their husbands' bodies but, you see, if we let 'em take 'em there'd soon be no palace left, *then* where would the king and queen live?"

The more poor Isis tried to make them believe her the more they thought her insane, so she tried a different approach, making friends with some of the queen's servants as they went to and fro about their errands. They were fascinated by the beautiful foreigner: her clothes, her make-up, the way she did her hair. Like the guards they found her story unbelievable, but they gossiped about her and one day the queen overheard them and asked to see this beautiful stranger.

This is exactly what Isis had hoped would happen. She was sent for and made herself so agreeable to the queen that Her Majesty took to the lovely Egyptian at once, even making her nurse to her baby son.

Isis was grateful for the queen's friendship, and resolved to do something for her. One night when the baby prince was sleeping, she cast a spell on him which would make him live for ever. For a few moments the baby was enveloped in magic fire, and it was at this instant that the queen decided to look in on her child. She knew nothing of the spell — what she saw was her baby on fire and seven scorpions in a circle round his crib, watching. Her screams brought servants running. Seeing the look of horror on the queen's face, Isis quickly broke the spell. The flames were snuffed out. The scorpions scuttled away. The baby was unharmed.

Isis comforted the queen. "The flames would not have hurt your son," she soothed. "They were part of a spell to make him immortal. Now the spell is broken and cannot be mended."

The queen looked at her. "You mean you can do *magic?*" she whispered.

Isis nodded.

The king, worried in case they had offended this powerful stranger, told her she should choose anything in his kingdom and it would be hers. At once she pointed to the great carved pillar. "I want that," she said.

Carpenters were sent for. The column was removed from its place and sawn lengthwise. Inside was the beautiful box, and in the box lay the body of Osiris. Everyone was amazed.

"So she's *not* mad after all," whispered the guards.

The king gave Isis a boat. Servants carried the box on board and secured it. Isis said goodbye to the queen, who was sad to see her go, and set sail for Egypt where she hid the precious box among the dense foliage of the delta. This done, she hurried to where she'd left the infant Horus, and was overjoyed to find that her spell had kept him safe.

LOVE TRIUMPHANT

Osiris lives again

*S*eth glared at the pig. "You claim to have important information and I hope for your sake it's true, because I don't usually grant audiences to pigs and I am partial to a slice or two of roast pork."

"Mighty One," squealed the pig, "I've uh … found the body of Osiris."

"You've *what?*"

"In the delta, Peerless One. While rooting."

"*Where* in the delta?"

"I … uh … I could take you to the place, Your Perfection."

"Then do it, pig. Do it *now* and I'll reward you. A title. Pig of Pigs. How's *that* sound?"

"Music to my ears, Your Supreme Divinity."

So Seth grabbed an axe and the pig led him to where the precious box lay concealed among reeds in the delta. Seth raised the lid, hauled out the body of Osiris and flung it on the ground.

"I know what she meant to do, that witch Isis," he grated. "She planned to have him restored to life. Well …" He raised his axe against the shimmering sky. "I'd like to see *anybody* restore him to life when I've finished with him."

The axe rose and fell, rose and fell, rose and fell again. When Seth stopped chopping, the body of Osiris lay in fourteen separate pieces. Laughing wildly, Seth picked up the pieces one by one and hurled them as far as he could into the Nile. "Goodbye, Osiris," he cackled. "Give my love to the crocodiles."

When Isis returned a few days later there was only the empty box.

"Where is Osiris?" she cried. "Who has taken him away?"

Weeping, she wandered the muddy labyrinth of the delta, asking the few people she met if they knew anything about the body's disappearance.

Little by little, from scraps of information picked up here and there she learned about the pig, the tyrant and the axe.

She was half mad with grief, but she was determined as well. She saw a picture inside her head of Seth laughing, and she whispered, "You think that's the end of us don't you, Seth? You think you're safe now on your golden throne, but you're not. You're *not*. I mean to find the pieces of Osiris, and when I do I'll beg the gods to bring him back to life. They'll do it – they can do anything. And then there's my son, Horus. Oh, he's just a child now but he's growing. Every day he grows stronger, here in the delta where your eyes don't see. Your eyes and your spies. Soon he'll be a man – a man with the power of the secret name of Ra. *Then* we shall see who laughs."

The brave sorceress took a sickle and began cutting reeds to make a flimsy boat. To her delight and amazement, her sister Nephthys came to help. Nephthys was married to Seth, but her husband's cruelties had so disgusted her that she had turned against him.

"He's mad," she told Isis, "a wild beast who has people tortured for his entertainment. If you'd *seen* him when he returned with that axe, the pig trotting at his heels. Pig of Pigs. He's got slaves building a *temple* to it. I don't know if I'll ever go back."

Side by side the sisters bound the long reeds in bunches and lashed the bunches together till the boat was finished. Then they climbed in and began paddling the craft in and out of the shallow, twisty creeks which made up the delta. As the boat skimmed along they peered down through the warm brown water, searching. It took a long time, but they found all the pieces of Osiris' body except one. The missing piece they would *never* find, because it had been eaten by a fish called the oxyrhynchus. Much later, when Isis' exile was over and the people of Egypt were told what the oxyrhynchus had done, they were appalled. From that day on, the oxyrhynchus was regarded as an unclean fish, and no Egyptian ever ate one again.

Isis and Nephthys laid the thirteen remaining pieces of Osiris on the ground and prayed to the mighty sun-god, Ra. He must have forgiven Isis for stealing his secret name, because he sent Thoth and Anubis, a god of the Underworld, to put the body together and breathe new life into it. When her beloved husband stirred and sat up, Isis was overcome with joy. She knelt and flung her arms round him, rejoicing at the strength in his muscles, the warmth of his skin. Now everything would be as it was before, and life would be perfect.

Alas, it was not to be.

"Isis," said Ra, "your husband lives again and for that you must be thankful, but he cannot remain in this world. I have appointed him Lord of the Land of the Dead, and there he will live for ever."

So the devoted couple were parted. They knew they would meet again in the realm of Thoth and Anubis when Isis' life was over, and with that they had to be content.

A
SERPENT
FROM SETH

The baby Horus saved

*T*here were times when Isis almost despaired of raising Horus to manhood. At any moment he might be bitten by a snake, stung by a scorpion or burnt up in one of the bushfires which sometimes raged through the sun-dried reeds. Her greatest fear was that Seth's spies would discover the infant and tell his cruel uncle where he was. To guard against this, the sorceress hid with Horus on a great floating island which was covered with reeds and papyrus plants, taller than a man. Because the island drifted from place to place, nobody could be sure where the fugitives might be from one day to the next.

Isis had to eat, so she couldn't stay with Horus all the time. Every now and then she would disguise herself as a poor woman of the marshes and go to beg food in one or other of the scattered villages. While she was gone, marsh-goddesses would surround the floating island and keep watch over the little boy. Sometimes the goddess Hathor came in the shape of a cow and fed him with her milk. Time was passing, and Horus was growing bigger and stronger every day.

One day, back in the city, Seth overheard a traveller talking about a wild child, born in the marshes and growing up like a savage in the reedbeds. The tyrant felt a pang of fear, sensing that this might be the child of Isis, and of Osiris whom he had murdered. He had the traveller seized and questioned, and the man said it was impossible to reach the child because of the marsh-goddesses. Seth made a plan. He had power over serpents, so he summoned a small, deadly snake and ordered it to the delta to kill the baby.

One day, while Isis was away begging, the snake eeled its way through the yellow water and slithered, unnoticed by the marsh-goddesses, on to the floating island. It found the infant sleeping in the reeds and bit him on the foot. The infant woke with a cry. The snake slid away through the papyrus stems as Horus began to scream. Deadly venom spread through the child's body so that when Isis returned, she found him dying.

She should have used her magic to save the child. She was a sorceress after all, but the sight of her stricken baby threw her into a panic. All she could do was stand with his shivering body in her arms and scream.

"Help!" she cried. "Will somebody please help me. My son is dying and I don't know what to do."

She looked about her wildly, willing somebody to appear but there was nobody. Osiris was in the Land of the Dead, and her sister Nephthys had had to return to the house of Seth because he was her husband. Isis paced back and forth among the reeds, screaming and wailing and rocking the child, who was growing weaker every minute.

Presently some fishermen heard the woman's cries and came to see what the matter was. They could see that Horus was gravely ill, but they didn't know what to do. One of them ran back to his reed boat and paddled swiftly to the nearest village, where a wise woman lived. He told her about the baby, and she returned with him to the floating island. She examined Horus, then turned to Isis.

"Your child has been bitten by a snake," she said. "No potion of mine can save him. Your only hope is to pray to Ra."

Isis glanced skyward. It was late afternoon. Ra's boat had almost reached the horizon. At any moment it would enter the rapids above the great cataract and be swept over and down, down into the abyss of Tuat. When that happened, night would fall and Ra would be on the Fields of Peace, unreachable till tomorrow. Seeing this, the sorceress threw back her head and let out the most desolate scream the world had ever heard.

So powerful was the sound that it echoed across the darkening sky and smacked like a wave on the side of Ra's boat, which stopped in midstream. Ra frowned and glanced about him, puzzled as to why his boat wouldn't go. No such thing had ever happened before. No such thing was possible. If the voyage didn't continue, night wouldn't fall. Everything on earth would stop. Tomorrow would never come.

Ra summoned Thoth and said, "Go down, to where that awful scream began. Find out what caused it. Quickly now."

Thoth flew to earth, tracing the scream to the floating island where Isis stood, rocking her baby.

"What is it?" he rapped. "You have halted the sun, destroyed time. Your scream has murdered tomorrow."

Isis glared at the ibis-headed god. "*Tomorrow?* Egypt will have no tomorrow if my baby dies. Seth knows this, and has sent a snake to kill him."

Thoth reached out and took the limp bundle from its mother's arms. He gazed into the baby's pale damp face and began muttering spells and incantations. "This child has the power of the secret name of Ra. He is under the protection of the Mighty One and no harm can befall him. The poison will leave him, leave him, leave him …"

As Thoth spoke the magic words, the watchers saw what looked like a tiny black snake wriggle out from between the infant's bluish lips, drop to the ground and melt away like smoke. At once Horus rallied, kicking in the god's arms, squalling lustily to be fed. Thoth handed him back to his ecstatic mother.

"Ra is watching this child," he murmured. "Nothing will harm him now."

Thoth returned to the sky. Ra's boat resumed its voyage. Night came. The fishermen slipped away. Isis fell asleep in a nest of reeds. The moon peered down and saw a smile on her lips, a bubble of milk on the baby's.

THE MAGIC EYE

How Horus lost his eye

*T*he followers of Seth never stopped searching for the son of Osiris, but Horus and his mother remained safe on their floating island. As her son grew, Isis told him stories about the cruelties of his uncle.

"He murdered your father," she'd say. "His own *brother*, so he wouldn't hesitate to kill you if he got the chance. You must stay away from him till the time is right."

Horus sighed. "You keep saying so, Mother, but when *will* the time be right? I'm big now, and strong. I could beat him, I *know* I could."

Isis shook her head. "Wait, my son. Be patient just a little longer and you *will* be king in Egypt."

But Horus was fed up with waiting. He was a bright, lively lad and there isn't much to do on a floating island in the Nile delta. He kept imagining the sort of life he'd be enjoying if he were king right now. Sport. Banquets. The latest fashions. Girls. He'd been patient long enough. He decided to give his mother the slip and go and challenge Seth without delay.

He left at night, striding across the moon-washed desert.

56

By morning he'd reached the royal palace. Seth recognised him at once by his brilliant magic eye. "Welcome, Nephew," he crooned. "To what do we owe this unexpected pleasure?"

"I've come to depose you, Uncle Seth," rapped Horus. "I *am* the rightful king after all."

Seth chuckled. "Depose *me*, impetuous youth? Still, I expect I was the same at your age. Join me in a glass of wine and we'll talk about it."

Horus was tired and thirsty and Seth seemed friendly enough. He followed his uncle into the palace, where the two of them sat down. Wine was brought, and food. They talked. More wine appeared. And more.

Every time Horus drained his cup it was refilled. He began to feel deliciously drowsy.

"Sho," he slurred, goggling at his genial host. Even his magic eye was bleary. "Wha' abou' this … this *crown* then, eh? Wha' about handing it over, Uncle Thes." He giggled. "I mean Uncle Ses. No." He frowned and shook his head. "I mean Uncle *Seth*."

The king smiled. "Poor boy. You're completely exhausted and no wonder, tramping across the desert all night. Why don't you have a nice long sleep now and we'll sort everything out tomorrow, eh?"

It sounded like a good idea. Horus was exhausted, and the wine fumes had driven his mother's oft-repeated warning out of his head. He allowed himself to be led to a cool dim bedchamber, where he collapsed on the bed and was instantly asleep.

It was midnight when Seth came creeping into the chamber and flung himself on his nephew. He'd hoped to kill the lad while he slept, but Horus woke with a cry and the pair fought, crashing to the floor and rolling about in a tangle of linen sheets. Seth clawed at his nephew's face, going for the magic eye. Horus kicked and struggled but Seth was relentless. He forced his thumb into the boy's eye-socket and gouged savagely.

"Let's see how tough you are without *this*," he gasped, ripping out the eye.

Horus screamed, broke away and scuttled into a corner of the room where he lay curled up, his hands clamped over the bleeding socket. With a cry of triumph Seth leapt to his feet, dashed the eye to the floor and trampled it.

So bright had the eye been that the instant it was destroyed, the night was plunged into a darkness more intense than ever before. The god Thoth saw this darkness descend and knew at once what was happening. He rushed to the palace, arriving as Seth was gathering himself to deliver the death blow to his stricken nephew.

"NO!" The king turned, wilting under the god's awful gaze. Thoth scooped up the pulped eye, made it whole again and restored it to Horus' face. As the youth rose, the darkness became less deep. Thoth used his awesome powers to heal both men. "Fight no more," he commanded. "There will be a trial at which the gods will decide which one of you will reign over Egypt."

Neither man was happy with this, but nobody defies Thoth and lives to tell the tale. Horus left the palace and headed back to the delta, and Seth sat wondering if he'd still be here when the trial was over. He hated the thought of being banished once more to the desert. In fact he vowed he'd never let it happen. "Thoth or no Thoth," he growled, but he took care not to say it too loudly.

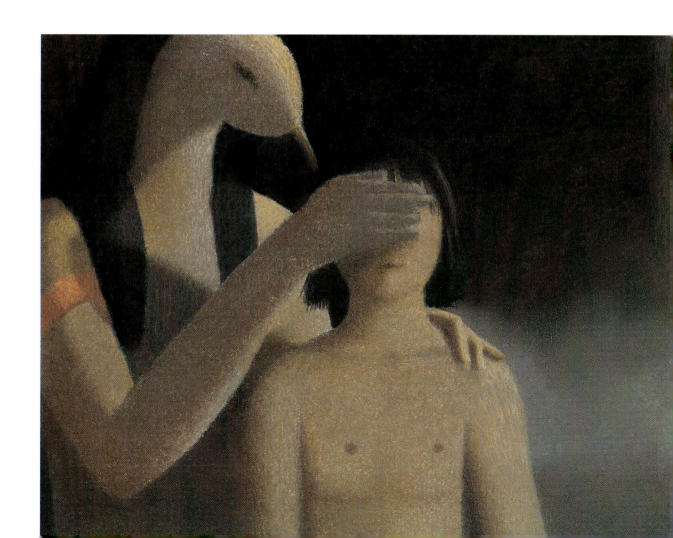

THE VENGEANCE OF HORUS

How Horus avenges the death of Osiris

*H*orus smiled grimly as he approached Heliopolis, where the trial would take place. Revenge is sweet, and the boy felt sure the gods were on his side. The moment he and Isis had longed for was at hand. The chief judge was the earth-god Geb, but every god and goddess of the Egyptians was there too. Seth and Horus were brought in.

Isis was the first witness. She told the court how she'd tracked down the murdered body of her husband Osiris, only to have Seth chop it up and throw the pieces in the river. She said Seth had taken the throne of Egypt from Osiris by force, and that the son of Osiris was the rightful heir. Shu, god of the air, nodded in agreement.

"Justice demands that Horus be king of Egypt."

Many of the gods thought so too, but Seth said, "I am stronger than Horus. I will make a better job of defending Egypt. If you don't believe me, let Horus come outside and fight me. If he wins, I'll give up my claim to the throne."

Thoth shook his head. "Horus doesn't need to fight you, Seth. The crown is his by right."

Some of the gods and goddesses agreed with this, but others weren't sure. Some thought Seth was best for Egypt because he was older and stronger. Others suggested that Seth might rule the south of the country while Horus ruled in the north. The argument swung back and forth. Time was passing. Presently it became obvious that the gods needed more time to decide, so Geb adjourned the proceedings.

"The court will meet again soon," he said.

Seth knew Horus was likely to win when the court reconvened. He said, "It's not fair. Horus has Isis to speak for him and everybody knows she's a powerful sorceress. I haven't got anybody like that to speak for me. I won't come to court again if Isis is going to be there."

The gods had a quick discussion and decided Seth was right. They banned Isis from all further meetings of the court. To make sure she didn't come, they chose an island in the river as their next meeting place.

When the day came, everybody crossed to the island by ferryboat. The ferryman had been warned not to let Isis on board his boat, but she used a spell to turn herself into a crippled old woman, and went up to him.

"Please, Mr Ferryman," she croaked, "my grandson is looking after cattle on the island and I've got this basket of food for him. Will you ferry me across?"

The ferryman shook his head. "I'm not ferrying any women today in case they're Isis in disguise."

Isis scoffed. "Do I *look* like a great sorceress to you, with my rags and my twisted leg? Come on – ferry me across and I'll give you a freshly baked cake from my basket."

It was the ferryman's turn to scoff. "D'you really think I'd risk the anger of the gods for one of your measly cakes? You're joking."

Isis looked at him. "What about a nice ring, then? Solid gold."

The ferryman's eyes gleamed greedily. "Show me."

Isis held out a withered hand. On the little finger was a thick gold ring.

The man licked his lips. "I get that if I ferry you across?"

Isis nodded.

"No trick? I mean, I don't have to do anything else?"

"Nothing else."

"And you're not Isis?"

"What do *you* think?"

"Give it me now, then."

Isis slipped the ring from her finger and dropped it in the ferryman's palm. He pocketed it and ferried the old woman across.

As soon as she was safely ashore, the sorceress cast another spell

which turned her into a beautiful young maiden. Seth was making his way towards the court when he spotted this lovely girl walking in the same direction. He stopped and waited for her. As she drew level he smiled and said, "You're very beautiful. Why don't the two of us find a bit of shade and talk?"

They sat down under a tree, where Isis immediately burst into tears.

"What's the matter?" asked Seth.

Isis shook her head. "I'm in the most awful trouble."

"Tell me about it," soothed Seth. "Perhaps I can help."

"Well," sniffled Isis, "it's like this. My husband died not long ago, leaving me with a fine son and some cattle. We would have managed all right, because we had a good house and my son could have looked after the animals, but then a cruel man came. He knew my husband was dead, so he threw us out of our home and threatened to beat my son if he tried to do anything. He's taken everything we owned and now we're penniless. Oh, sir ..." She gazed at Seth through her tears. "You're obviously an important man. D'you think you could ...?"

"Of course!" Seth leapt to his feet. "Show me this man. This scoundrel. I'll teach him to treat you cruelly and to rob your son of his rightful inheritance. I'll beat him with my club. I'll throw him out of your house and kick him halfway across Egypt. How *dare* he use violence to rob honest folk and leave them destitute?"

As Seth ranted on, Isis turned herself into a bird and flew up into the tree.

"It's you!" she screeched. "*You* are that man. You have left me destitute and robbed my son Horus of his rightful inheritance. Why don't you kick *yourself* halfway across Egypt?"

A crowd of gods and goddesses, who had come to see what all the noise was about, burst out laughing.

Seth, weeping with rage, glared at them.

"It isn't fair!" he choked. "She tricked me and she's not even supposed to *be* here." They laughed louder. "You promised!" They went on laughing. "Well at *least* punish that rotten ferryman. It's all his fault."

The gods agreed with Seth about the greedy ferryman. He was seized, and all his toes were cut off. It hurt, and afterwards his shoes didn't fit. He wished he had never set eyes on the solid gold ring.

When they finally got into court, most of the gods and goddesses were in favour of giving the crown to Horus. Seth shook with rage.

"Give him the crown and I'll rip it from his head!" he cried. "I'll put him in the Nile like his father before him. Let him *fight* me to see who rules Egypt."

"Very well," said Horus. "I'll fight him."

They went down to the river. There, Seth turned himself into a great hippopotamus and plunged into the water. Horus got into a boat. Isis went with him. When the hippo surfaced, intent on capsizing the boat, Horus struck at it with a harpoon of copper, wounding the beast. The hippo backed off, then came surging in again. If Seth could knock Horus into the water, the boy would be at the mercy of his deadly tusks. Again Horus lunged, and once more the harpoon found its mark. The waters frothed red as Seth struggled to tear free of the copper barbs. Seven times Horus stabbed the hippo, and still it came back at the boat.

Horus could see only one way of stopping his opponent. Plunging into the river himself, he became a hippo. The two mighty beasts clashed in a welter of bloody froth, lunging and snapping at each other's flanks with fearsome tusks. Many wounds were inflicted, but neither would yield so they changed shapes, fighting each other as bulls, as lions, as crocodiles. Flesh was ripped. Bones broken. Still neither man would yield. Eighty years went by and still the fight continued. Eighty years isn't very long to gods because they live for ever, but it was boring because neither fighter seemed to be winning.

The gods and goddesses started yawning and looking for something to take their minds off the fight. One or two dozed off. It was obvious that neither contestant was going to give in. Finally Ra left the Fields of Peace and came in person to settle the matter.

"Seth," he said, "Osiris was an innocent man and you murdered him. Therefore Horus is in the right and you are in the wrong. Let Horus reign over Egypt." He looked at Seth. "You," he said, "will come and live with me in the sky. I'll appoint you god of storms, so that people will always fear you." Ra knew that Seth liked to cause fear.

So Horus became king of Egypt like his father before him, and with Isis to advise him he ruled wisely and well. Peace and prosperity settled over the land. Everybody said it was just like the reign of Osiris, which isn't surprising since both kings had the same adviser. Everybody was content. Well no – not *everybody*. Seth didn't care for the arrangement, but he didn't dare defy Ra. He became god of storms and grumbled about it, and his grumbling was heard as thunder in the skies above the land he'd stolen and lost.

THE PRINCE AND THE PHANTOMS

The magic book of Thoth

*G*ods are not happy when men seek godlike powers and Thoth, the Measurer of Time, was no exception. Thoth possessed much secret knowledge essential to the working of magic, and mortal magicians were always looking for ways to get this knowledge from him.

Once a prince called Setna Khaemwese, who fancied himself a magician, learned that a book of magic written by Thoth lay buried in an ancient tomb near the city of Memphis. He resolved to go there and steal it. Stealing from graves was an offence punishable by death, so he was taking a terrible risk.

He travelled to Memphis, found out through discreet inquiry where the tomb lay and approached it warily, keeping a lookout for guards, but it seemed nobody was guarding the place. Strange, he thought, since it contains a precious book many would kill to own.

In the doorway he paused, glanced all around to make sure nobody was watching and slipped inside. It was dark and cold and many unseen objects littered the floor, causing him to stumble. The place felt haunted and the prince was frightened. He lit the small lamp he had brought with him and began searching for the book, trying not to think about ghosts. He'd just located it and was reaching out to grab it when a troupe of ghastly phantoms materialised.

"Before you touch that book," groaned a particularly loathsome apparition, "look at us. Each one of us was once a living man like you. We wished to be great magicians, so we banded together and stole that book from a chest at the bottom of the Nile."

"And then … what?" croaked the prince.

"And then Thoth killed us all," sighed the ghost. "He *knows*, you see. He always knows, and now it is our miserable fate to haunt this cold dark tomb for ever and guard the book. We cannot let you take it."

That might have been the end of the story, except that the prince had come armed with certain potent amulets: charms with powers to ward off spirits. He produced these amulets, held them aloft in the lamplight. The ghosts sighed and rustled and fell back, melting into the shadowy corners of the tomb.

The young man seized the magic book and began walking slowly backwards, taking care to keep the amulets always between himself and the ghosts. Even with their protection he was terrified, and he sobbed with relief when he felt the doorway at his back. Outside he quickly recovered, tucked the book under his arm and started for home feeling mightily pleased with himself.

He hadn't gone far when he saw a beautiful young woman approaching. Her eyes were dark and lustrous, her mouth reminded him of crushed sweet berries and the moonlight made a diadem of her hair. As a prince he had seen many beautiful women, but none so flawless as this. He fell instantly and helplessly in love. "I'd do anything for your sake," he groaned. "*Anything*."

"Very well," said the vision of loveliness crisply. "Give me all your fortune."

"Gladly," gasped Setna, and he did.

"Now order your children killed."

"A trifle," murmured the prince, and ordered them killed at once.

"And now," breathed the beauty, "you may hold me."

The prince's eager arms encircled the girl's soft body, but no sooner had the couple settled themselves on the ground than the girl vanished. Setna found himself lying naked in the middle of a road. He leapt up with a cry of despair.

"What have I done?" he cried. "My children … oh, my poor children."

He ran all the way home, sobbing and gasping, to find his children completely unharmed. He knew then that the beautiful woman had been a phantom sent by Thoth, and that, had the god so wished, his fortune would be gone and his children dead.

Without pausing even to refresh himself, the prince hurried back to Memphis and returned the magic book to its place in the tomb. From that day on he was a prince to his people and a father to his children, content to leave magic to the gods.

THE ANGRY GOD

Why the Nile stopped flooding

One year, in the reign of King Djoser, the river Nile didn't rise. The fields dried out for lack of water, no fresh silt was deposited and the harvest was poor.

"Oh, well," said the Egyptians, who had seen poor harvests before, "we'll just have to eat less and wait for next year's flood."

But a year passed and the river failed again. Under the burning sun the soil turned to dust, which the wind blew away. The people grew thin and listless. The cattle were skin and bone.

Seven times the Nile failed to rise. After seven years of famine there were almost no cattle left, and the Egyptians themselves were starting to die.

King Djoser was desperate. He sent for his architect, Imhotep, who had a reputation as a healer and magician.

"Why has the Nile stopped flooding?" he asked.

Imhotep shook his head. "I do not know, Mighty One, but I will try to find out."

He shut himself away and spent some days poring over his

books of magic. Presently he approached the king and said, "Mighty One, it seems there is a spirit named Hapy. He lives in two caverns under the island of Elephantine on the Upper Nile, and he is the spirit of the flood. Seven years ago something bad happened up there. The ram-god Khnum entered the caverns and imprisoned Hapy. Now Khnum controls the cavern doors. Only he can unbolt them and let the waters flow, and he isn't doing it. Perhaps he is angry with us."

When he heard this, King Djoser ordered his priests to make lavish offerings to Khnum. No expense was to be spared. That night Khnum came to the king in a dream, promising to release Hapy. Next day the Nile flooded. The fields were irrigated. Green shoots came thrusting through the silt. Imhotep's wisdom had saved his people.

THE KING WHO HAD EVERYTHING

The lost clasp

*K*ing Sneferu of Egypt had everything a man could want and he was bored, bored, bored. He was bored with his riches, his wives and his life in the palace. He was fed up with signing decrees, granting audiences and being carried, dripping with gold, in processions. He was so bored that he was bored with being bored.

One day he sent for his chief wise man, whose name was Djadja-em-ankh. "I'm bored," he said, "and you are wise. Think of a way to amuse and entertain me, or I shall go mad."

Djadja-em-ankh thought for a minute. "What you need," he said, "is a bit of fresh air and exercise."

"Boring!" snapped the king.

The wise man shook his head. "Not if we go down to the lake," he said.

The palace grounds had its own magnificent lake, with trees and lawns and every sort of wildfowl. Sneferu was about to say boring again when his wise man continued.

"Mighty One, you could sit by the lakeside, and I'd arrange

for a boatful of Egypt's loveliest girls to be on the water, and they'd row backwards and forwards in front of you with hardly anything on."

Sneferu was fond of girls with hardly anything on. His eyes lit up as he pictured the scene.

"Yes!" he cried, "and I could pick one out to keep me company this evening in my chambers."

So the king, feeling better already, sent for his outdoor clothes while Djadja-em-ankh hurried round to the harem to arrange for the girls. He selected twenty of the youngest and most curvaceous and told them to wear only nets of beads. At the royal boathouse he chose a handsome craft and ordered its oars to be covered with gold leaf.

While all this was going on, King Sneferu was dressed by slaves, installed on a palanquin and carried down to the lake. It would probably have done him good to walk, but Pharaohs don't. Slaves had set up a comfortable chair for their master at the water's edge. Sneferu was helped down from the palanquin and into the chair, where he sat taking deep breaths and gazing out across the water. The boat appeared almost at once, gliding over the cool bright surface, its oars glittering in the sun.

The wise man appeared at the king's elbow. "Well, Mighty One; what do you think?"

The king's eyes followed the boat as it passed before him.

"Gorgeous," he breathed. "Beautiful. Tell them to row closer to the shore next time – they're a bit far out."

Djadja-em-ankh passed on the king's order and the boat returned, its oar-blades brushing the lakeside reeds.

"Perfect," sighed the king.

As the boat skimmed back and forth, the king noticed that one of the girls kept fiddling with the turquoise clasp which held her hair in place. She was even lovelier than her companions, and Sneferu was about to point her out to the wise man as his choice for the evening, when the clasp she was playing with slipped from her fingers and fell into the water.

At once the girl stopped rowing and the boat slowed.

"What's happening?" demanded Sneferu. "Why have they stopped?"

Djadja-em-ankh leaned forward. "The girl has lost her hair-clasp in the water, Mighty One."

"Oh – tell her I'll give her another," snapped the king, "a better one, only get the boat moving again."

The wise man conveyed the king's offer to the girl, but she shook her head.

"I don't want another one," she protested, "I want *mine*."

Djadja-em-ankh wondered whether she realised her pretty head might easily join the clasp at the bottom of the lake if the king didn't see movement in a minute. No sooner had he thought this than the king called out, "Now what's the matter?"

"Er – the girl wants her *own* clasp, Mighty One."

"Oh, well." The mighty one flapped a hand. "This whole thing was your idea. *You* sort it out, only make it snappy."

Luckily, the wise man was a bit of a magician. He spoke a powerful spell, and an amazing thing happened. The waters of the lake parted, rearing up in a wall to reveal its muddy bed and the hair-clasp lying there.

The king gasped, bending forward in his chair to witness the miracle.

"Wow!" he breathed, "and to think this morning I was bored!"

Swiftly Djadja-em-ankh stepped on to the mud, retrieved the clasp and restored it to its owner. Then he stood on the bank and uttered another spell. At once the wall of water crashed down, covering the lakebed. A flock of startled wildfowl exploded into flight. Wavelets surged towards the king's feet, gurgling among the reeds. The king shouted with glee.

In minutes, the lake's surface was calm once more. The girls bent to their oars. The boat sliced through the water. The king sat back with a sigh. There'd be feasting tonight. Feasting, and the girl with the turquoise clasp.

TREACHEROUS WIVES

A faithful brother

Among the people who farmed the rich soil on the banks of the Nile were two brothers, Bata and Anpu. Anpu owned the farm because he was older than Bata, but Bata didn't mind. He was a gentle, easygoing man, happy to help Anpu with the work. Bata was very strong, and he understood the speech of animals. He slept in the barn so that Anpu and his wife could share the bedroom, and he did most of the heavy lifting about the farm.

One day while the brothers were out sowing corn, they ran out of seed. Anpu turned to his brother.

"Go back to the house and fetch more seed," he ordered. The day was very hot and he didn't fancy humping sacks of corn himself.

"All right," said Bata, who never complained. "I shan't be long."

When he arrived at the house he saw his brother's wife sitting on the ground, plaiting her long black hair.

"Go to the store," he told her, "and fetch out some seed-corn."

"Can't you see I'm busy?" snapped the woman. "Fetch it yourself."

Bata shrugged and walked round to the store. He was back a minute later carrying three sacks of wheat and two of barley. Anpu's wife gazed at him, admiring his muscular body.

"Why don't you put down those sacks and come and sit beside me for a while?" she smiled. "We could talk and kiss and . . . you know?"

Bata looked at her in amazement. "You're my brother's wife," he growled. "I wouldn't dream of kissing and cuddling with you. It wouldn't be right."

"Please yourself," sulked the woman. "Take your silly sacks and get out of my sight. Die of sunstroke for all I care."

When Bata had gone, the woman grew afraid. Suppose Bata told Anpu what she'd suggested? She got some dark grease from a lamp and rubbed it into her skin to make herself look bruised. She messed up her hair too, and tore her dress. Then she lay on the bed, groaning.

When Anpu came home at sunset she said, "Bata attacked me. He wanted to kiss and cuddle me but I said no, so he attacked me."

Anpu was furious. He seized a spear and stood behind the door.

Bata was bringing the cows home. Anpu meant to spear his brother as he came in the door, but one of the cows said, "Bata, your brother is waiting behind the door to kill you. His wife has told him you attacked her." Bata fled with Anpu hot on his heels.

As he ran, Bata prayed to the mighty sun-god, Ra. "I am innocent," he cried. "Save me from my brother's wrath."

Ra, who can do anything, caused a river to open up between the brothers. The river had crocodiles. Anpu stopped, glaring at his brother across the water. Bata stopped too, and called across.

"Your wife lied to you. She invited me to kiss her and I refused. She was angry, so she made up the story about my attacking her. I swear I never touched her."

Anpu shook his head. "You're lying, Brother. My wife would never make up a story like that."

"If I'm guilty," answered Bata, "why has Ra caused this river to appear between us?"

Anpu was silent for a moment. He knew Ra wouldn't intervene to protect a guilty man, so his brother must be telling the truth.

"All right," he said, "I believe you. Come on home."

"No." Bata shook his head. "It wouldn't be the same. I'll find a place of my own." He turned and walked away.

Anpu was both angry and sad. He carried his spear back to the farm and killed his wife with it.

Bata walked for many days, till he came to the Valley of the Pine in the land of Syria. His heart ached constantly from missing his brother and everybody he knew, so he plucked it out and hid it among the branches of the great pine tree, then set about building a house. He tilled the soil and hunted to feed himself, but he was lonely. Ra took pity on his loneliness and ordered the god Khnum to make him a wife. Khnum did so, and she was one of the most beautiful women on earth. Her name was Bintnefer, and Bata was so delighted with her that he worried in case something should happen to her.

He said, "Bintnefer, you are very precious to me. Therefore you must promise me that you will never stray too close to the water when you walk beside the sea, for you might be swept away by a wave." Their house was very close to the sea.

"I'm not a child," snapped Bintnefer. "I can take care of myself."

"You are not a child but you are my wife," retorted Bata, "and it is a

wife's duty to obey her husband. If you withhold your promise, you will be locked inside the house whenever I am away."

"Oh, very well," sulked Bintnefer, "I promise." But she didn't intend to keep her word.

One day not long afterwards she deliberately walked very close to the water, and sure enough a great wave came racing up the sand and overtook her, swirling round her so that she almost fell over. She managed to regain her balance, but the wave tore out a lock of her magnificent hair and carried it away to sea.

Presently the lock of hair was washed up on the shores of Egypt, at a spot where Pharaoh's washermen washed clothes in the sea. They took the hair to the king, who was amazed at its beauty and fragrance. He dispatched servants to every known land to search for the owner of the hair.

"When you find her," he ordered, "bring her to me at once."

Pharaoh's servants travelled far and wide. Now and then one would find his way to the Valley of the Pine, but Bata was always watching and killed anyone who came near. One day, a servant set eyes on Bintnefer and managed to flee before Bata could catch him. This servant returned to Egypt and told the king where she was to be found.

Straightaway, Pharaoh sent a detachment of soldiers to Syria. With the soldiers he sent an old woman who carried a bagful of fine jewellery. The soldiers marched into the Valley of the Pine and kept Bata busy while the old woman showed Bintnefer what was in her bag.

"Return with me to Egypt," she crooned, "and all of this is yours."

Bintnefer was not a particularly good wife and the jewels tempted her. She told the old woman where her husband's heart was hidden. The soldiers cut down the pine tree and Bata fell dead. The soldiers returned in triumph to Egypt and Bintnefer became Pharaoh's chief wife and queen of Egypt.

Meanwhile Anpu, who had been missing his brother, traced him to the Valley of the Pine. He found the tree cut down and Bata lying dead. He searched around till he found his brother's shrivelled heart, which he placed in a bowl of water. At once there stood before him a magnificent bull.

"I am your brother Bata," said the bull. "I want you to take me to Egypt and present me to Pharaoh as a gift."

Anpu did as his brother asked. Pharaoh was delighted with the bull, ordering it to be kept within the palace grounds and given the best of care.

One day the bull contrived to approach Bintnefer as she strolled alone in the garden, a thing she had promised Pharaoh she would never do.

"Do you not know me, Bintnefer?" it asked.

The queen gazed haughtily at the creature.

"I am queen of Egypt," she said, "I don't know *any* beasts."

"Then allow me to introduce myself," replied the bull. "I am Bata, the husband you betrayed."

Bintnefer squealed and fled, and from that day on she lived in fear. Why had Bata come here? What did he mean to do?

The next time Pharaoh feasted with his queen, she waited till he'd had a lot to drink and asked him to grant her a wish. He agreed, and she asked for the bull's liver to eat. Pharaoh was angry and upset, but a promise is a promise. The bull was slaughtered and its liver given to Bintnefer.

As the bull died, two drops of blood fell beside the palace gates and grew into two beautiful trees. Pharaoh was delighted, but the queen knew that the trees contained the spirit of Bata and demanded that they be cut down and made into furniture for her chamber. As woodcutters chopped at the two trunks, a splinter flew into Bintnefer's mouth. She swallowed it, and straight away a baby started to grow inside her. In due time the queen gave birth to a son, and when Pharaoh died some years later the child became king. He ascended Pharaoh's golden throne and had his mother brought before him.

"Mother," he said, as she knelt at his feet, "I am Bata, the husband you betrayed *three* times: as man, bull and tree. Justice has caught up with you at last, and now you will die."

Begging and weeping, the faithless queen was dragged away and executed. Bata sent for Anpu his brother and made him a member of the royal family, and when Bata died after a prosperous thirty-year reign Anpu succeeded him as Pharaoh.

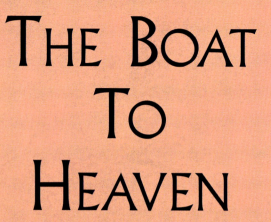

THE BOAT TO HEAVEN

A dread voyage

*W*hile Anpu was being hailed as Egypt's new Pharaoh, his brother's spirit or *Ka* was setting out on a dread voyage. It was a voyage every Egyptian had to face after death if he hoped to dwell for ever with the gods on the Fields of Peace.

The voyage began in the black waters of the abyss known as Tuat, which was the gateway to the Underworld. The waters of the Celestial Nile crashed unceasingly into the abyss, and at the end of each day Ra's sun-boat was swept over the lip of the cataract and down, down into the foaming waters. Ra was never on board, because he always stepped out on to the Fields of Peace before the vessel plunged over the edge, but a part of his spirit remained with the boat to help the spirits of the dead.

So it was that Bata found himself thrashing in thundering black waters which tossed him to and fro and threatened to drown him. He could see nothing, yet he knew he was not alone. Other spirits struggled all around, while beneath the roiling surface lurked enormous crocodiles whose food was the spirits of the wicked, whom they would seize and pull under before they could scramble aboard Ra's boat.

It seemed to the choking Bata that aeons passed before the vessel came, but at last there it was, rocking wildly. He flailed his way towards it and, with the last of his strength, hauled himself aboard. As he lay gasping like a landed fish in the bottom of the boat, it came to him that here in Tuat all were equal. Around him and on top of him lay farmers, servants, peasant women, panting and spluttering and paying no heed to the man who yesterday was their Pharaoh. He realised that on *this* voyage it wouldn't matter how great or how lowly the travellers had been. The only thing that mattered now was how they'd *lived* their lives – how they'd behaved towards others, especially the helpless and those in need. Only those spirits which were heavy with good deeds had any hope of completing the voyage.

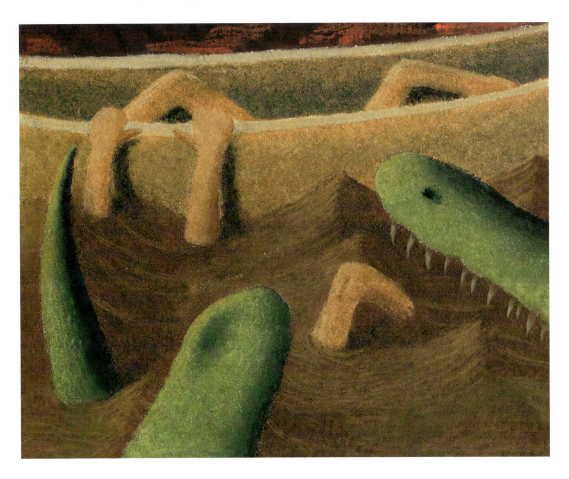

As Bata pondered these things, the boat was swept by the current through a dark gateway into the terrible valley of Amantet. He knew that Amantet is divided into twelve regions, one for each hour of the night. He knew that each region is guarded by stout doors, and that snakes of enormous length and thickness lie along ledges, waiting to throw their loathsome coils about the spirits of the unworthy. He knew that these poor wretches are crushed and swallowed, their existence snuffed out for ever, while their more worthy companions sail on towards the faraway dawn. He drew a deep breath, picked himself up and prepared for the struggle.

The first five divisions of Amantet were traversed by Bata in blood and anguish and the boat, less crowded now, entered the sixth and most dreadful division, known as the Hall of Osiris, Judge of the Dead. Bata knew that here not even the protection of the mighty Ra could help him, for this was the realm of the gods of the Underworld. Here, each voyager

would be questioned by forty-two gods. Here, each heart would be weighed against the weight of a feather. For some, this hall would prove to be journey's end.

On a raised platform at the farthest end of the hall sat Osiris on a golden throne. His wife Isis stood at his right hand, his sister Nephthys at his left. Before him knelt Anubis, the jackal-headed god who kept the scales in which hearts are weighed. Thoth, scribe of the gods, stood by to record the result of the weighing. Ranged around the walls were forty-two thrones of ivory and gold, and on each of these sat a god or goddess. Between the scales and the throne of Osiris yawned a bottomless pit, the lair of a monster which waited to devour those whose hearts are light with lack of good deeds.

One by one the terrified voyagers would be led to the centre of the hall to be interrogated by the forty-two gods, and it fell to Bata to go first. A falcon-headed god glared at him.

"Did you murder?"

"Never, Divinity."

Another god cleared his throat. "*Thieve* then – did you ever thieve?"

"No, Divinity."

"What about dishonouring the gods?" probed a catlike goddess.

Bata shook his head. "I always honoured the gods, Divinity."

"Very well," boomed Osiris, "let him approach the scales."

Trembling, Bata was led by Horus, son of Osiris, to stand before the terrible scales. Here his heart was plucked from his body and placed in the pan. If it outweighed the feather or balanced it exactly, he would pass. If the feather sank he would be grabbed and thrown headlong into the pit. He knew that protestations, pleas for mercy would fall on deaf ears. In the Hall of Osiris there is no appeal.

Bata had been a wise and a gentle Pharaoh. His heart was heavy with good deeds, so that it easily outweighed the feather. Faint with relief he was escorted back to Ra's boat, bobbing on black water in the seventh division of Amantet, but many of his companions had led less virtuous lives and these he never saw again. From this point on the voyage would be easier, because those on board knew they had the strength and the virtue to overcome all the loathsome enemies they would meet.

In the twelfth and last division they faced the most awful beast of all: a serpent so thick that its body blocked the entire width of the stream. The boat couldn't possibly get past this creature: the only way was to go *through* it. As the boat lurched between the gaping jaws past the razor fangs, down the red gullet and on through the black, stinking gut Bata cried out in fear, convinced that not even a virtuous spirit could survive this, but he and his remaining companions were under the protection of the awesome Ra, and at last they glimpsed light ahead. The light swelled, growing more and more brilliant till the boat emerged into the glory of a golden dawn. Bata's ordeal was over. He and his ecstatic companions disembarked on to the Fields of Peace, where they would live for ever.

Ra stepped into his boat. On earth, a new day began.

THE GODS AND GODDESSES IN THESE STORIES

The stories of the gods of ancient Egypt come from very fragmented sources: carvings or inscriptions in temples or tombs or written on papyri buried with the wealthy dead. As the civilisation of ancient Egypt lasted more than three thousand years, the stories handed down through all that time inevitably went through many changes, as did the gods and goddesses themselves.

The gods and goddesses were usually shown in paintings and sculptures with the heads of animals or birds, but in the stories they often changed their heads from animal to human form, or even transformed themselves completely into animals.

The Rosetta Stone discovered in the early nineteenth century was a most important find enabling scholars to decipher ancient Egyptian writing or hieroglyphs. The stone is made of hard black basalt on which is carved finely cut writing in three scripts: the top third consists of hieroglyphs, the middle is Demotic (a joined-up version of the ancient Egyptian script) and the bottom section is classical Greek. As scholars could easily read the Greek script, they were able to translate the hieroglyphs and so unlock many of the secrets of ancient Egyptian inscriptions, including stories of all the great gods and goddesses.

AMON
Alternative name for the sun god Ra.

ANUBIS
A god of the Underworld in charge of tombs and mummies. He is usually represented in the form of a seated jackal or a man with a jackal's head.

GEB
The god of the earth whose sister and wife was Nut the sky goddess. He was the son of Shu and Tefnut and the father of Osiris, Isis, Seth and Nephthys and therefore one of the chief gods.

HAPY
The god of the Nile flood. He symbolised the people's dependence on the Nile to bring water and fertile soil to grow their crops.

HATHOR
The goddess of love and motherhood. She is often represented as a cow, or as a woman wearing a headdress of cow's horns between which is held a sun disc.

HORUS
The god of the sky and son of Osiris and Isis who was also seen as the protector of the reigning pharaoh. Usually shown as a hawk or as a man with the head of a hawk.

ISIS
The powerful sorceress and goddess wife and sister of Osiris. Also the mother of Horus. She is said to have made the first mummy from the dead body of Osiris.

KHEPERA
The creator and father of the gods usually depicted in the form of a scarab or dung beetle.

KHEPHRI
Alternative name for the sun god Ra.

KHNUM
A potter god thought to have created mortals from clay. Often represented as a man with a ram's head, he is mainly associated with the Nile flood and fertile soil.

NEPHTHYS
A goddess of the dead, the wife and sister of Seth and mother of Anubis. She was also the sister of Isis and helped in the search for the dead Osiris.

NUT
The daughter of Shu and goddess of the sky. Also the sister and wife of Geb and mother of Osiris, Isis, Nephthys and Seth. Nut's body was thought to be arched over the earth.

OSIRIS
One of the most important gods in ancient Egypt, he showed the people how to farm. He was also a god of the dead and the Underworld, brother and husband of Isis, and father of Horus.

PTAH
Alternative name for the sun god Ra.

RA
The sun god and greatest of all the gods who was thought to be a creator of both gods and mortals. Also called Amon, Ptah or Khephri according to where he was worshipped. Usually represented as a hawk-headed human figure often with a sun disc headdress.

SEKHMET
Lioness goddess of death and destruction.

SETH
The god of chaos and confusion, son of the sky goddess Nut and jealous brother of Osiris. When the throne of Egypt was returned to Horus, Ra made Seth god of storms.

SHU
The god of the air and sunlight. His role was to support the outstretched figure of the sky goddess Nut, separating her from the earth god Geb.

TEFNUT
The daughter of Ra and goddess of dew and rain. She was wife and sister to Shu and mother of Geb and Nut. Shu and Tefnut were the first gods created by Ra.

THOTH
The god of writing and knowledge, scribe to the gods and a god of the Underworld. He was also lord of the moon and god of wisdom. Often represented with the head of an ibis.